CW00695238

Gallery Books
Editor Peter Fallon

WASHING UP

Derek Mahon

WASHING UP

Gallery Books

Washing Up
was first published
simultaneously in paperback
and in a clothbound edition
in October 2020.
Reprinted 2021.

The Gallery Press
Loughcrew
Oldcastle
County Meath
Ireland
www.gallerypress.com

ISBN 978 1 91133 790 4

A CIP catalogue record for this book
is available from the British Library.

Washing Up receives financial assistance
from the Arts Council.

Contents

for Sarah

The Old Place

for Hugo and Eliza Duff

This is for when you're older and no longer
chasing around the gardens after rabbits
gone from the hutch, but working for exams
and learning how to drive; this is for when
you've become even bigger and stronger
than you are now, acquired adult habits
and started practising the grown-up games.
It will be time enough to read it then

and recall, briefly, the old author of it
framed in the window at his writing table
who was at peace here in a world ill-at-ease
with itself, its past, a future yours to know —
a sort of hermit, working not for profit,
who was content to engage those few notable
readers who saw the point of the exercise.
You've other things on your minds, but even so.

Believe me, everything will be all right
as far as you're concerned, for you were born
to many blessings in this temperate zone
and grew like roses in rain and sunlight,
putting out leaves as in a time-lapse film.
Thriving and shining in the natural realm,
earth spirits, creatures of the wood, you two
are probably all set up in cities now —

but think at times of your own special space,
the weathered cherub and blunt lion face
watching for you however far you go
and musing on the life of the old place;
for this is where the veiled influences

hide out in secret springs and undergrowth
familiar to initiates' heightened senses
as to your own in your enchanted youth.

Atlantis

There are still songs to be sung beyond the human.
                          — Paul Celan

— These heard above the seismic turbulence
as when a blue whale or a giant squid
decides to emerge from its mysterious depth;
but this is a stranger miracle, intense
tectonic granite dripping with seaweed,
gemmed with barnacles like a salvaged ship.

Think of it, risen from the sea, streaming
with sea water, its now gleaming surfaces
of new leaf and clean slate there for us
and our designs — island or continent
drying out in the wind — a new Atlantis
ripe with promise (I must be dreaming)

where we can plant our ideal society;
a coral shoreline fringed with cloud forest,
or a lost civilization, its architecture
waiting to be replaced by the white city
and wide roads of a fresh infrastructure:
poured concrete, aluminium, only the best.

Still faintly audible there, dwindling stars,
those angel voices singing in the light
eternal, but drowned out by rock and radios
tuned to the one frequency at all hours,
besides the construction racket day and night,
incoming email keeping us on our toes —

these to be heard still by the post-human.
The wised-up robots who do the real work
even in the service industries after dark

perform with more than natural acumen
while we relax in deckchairs on balconies
sipping tequila in an evening breeze.

There will be cruise ships, the last savages
banished to caves and cabins, dubious sentiments
silenced, and the few relics of past ages
quickly recycled so no trace survives
of anything not in the future tense;
the sun will smile upon our perfect lives.

It smiles already on this shining myth,
pipe dream, cloud castle, blest Land of Cocaine,
the young in charge, the old folks young again,
with its strip mining and data mining both
thriving, and globalization kicking in.
It will be fabulous and will cost the earth.

Alone in the Dark

1

We're neither of us as young as we were once
but you've no reason to resist the chance
of a few drinks in town, a girls' night out.
Come back *sober*, or only *slightly* tight;
but don't let that inhibit your sublime
subversion of the dominant male paradigm.

I vaguely picture a seditious clique
of drunken floozies laughing themselves sick.
You and your serious women friends meanwhile,
sipping the wine in rather elegant style,
will be conspiring about how to find
funds for the arts, and topics of that kind.

Don't put the light on; let me rack my brains
for some *key* as the summer night convenes,
setting tight-fisted private enterprise
against the open-handed evening skies
with a pale moon governing time and tide,
its sphere of influence reaching far and wide.

Selene's daughters, at a dim corner table
in the Blue Haven, may your unanswerable
insights light the world in the same fashion,
your laughter banishing mere calculation.
Go and have fun; me, having finished work,
I can just sit alone here in the dark.

2

Alone now in the dark, I strive to check
routine emergence of an old dislike
for the triumphant kitsch on every side.
The only sure escape is to be dead;
but maybe if I ignore the latest news,
the opinion pieces, and take longer views . . .

A longer view might see the world transformed,
harsh masters of the universe disarmed,
the *faux* democracies deprived of air,
disgrace of the fat giants everywhere;
no more hedge funds, no more 'derivatives'
or high-tech requisition of real lives.

Though it's been said a thousand times before
what is required of us is something more,
something as obvious as a change of heart.
Too much to ask, of course, but we could start
with a new angle on the life we know
like a spring growth beginning under snow

or a stream glittering on a bed of stones;
but these examples are the familiar ones.
The arts you talk about, the song and dance,
point to the same end and the same advance,
each one a more than adequate epiphany;
and the clear evidence of an evening sky.

3

Alone in the dark here, I can still make out
the glimmering white paper where I write
by the fierce radiance of a single star
audibly buzzing, visibly sparkling there,
its vibrant energy spent long ago
but still apparent to the world below.

Bright star, the guiding light of vanished youth,
whose cold intensity reflected truth
and represented an extinct ideal
of perfect shining on the conditional,
you shine for me tonight in my old age,
still cold and bright on the unfinished page.

What earthly use, though? No fine words of mine
will save the drowned child at the waterline
or a condemned forest from the chainsaw;
and yet there's an old supernatural law
that says the imagination, once in play,
can work strange miracles from day to day.

So help me broadcast the poetic word,
bright star, among the cynical and bored,
the populations sold out to material
interests, the unreality of the 'real' . . .
It's getting late; but suddenly I hear
your footstep, and a key turns in the door.

Natural Resources

When there is no more oil on tap
we will return to paper wrap;
deprived of aviation fuel,
flight will be a dirigible
and the antique combustion engine,
petrol exhausted, run on gin.

Natural Selection

The great beech more than two centuries old,
its heavy branches reaching far and wide,
came down last year in a cyclone and, behold,
next spring the others it had overgrown
had grown the faster, lightened and enskied
towards the reviving, now available sun.

Natural selection saved the slighter beech.
The unsustainable one laid low at last
by changing climate, storms on the rampage,
we its near neighbours rise into the breach,
the bright gap, only to repeat the past —
dying, us too, of gravity and old age.

But we survive for now, expanding quick
after a shadowy life in part protected
from windy weather, 'leafy hands' outspread
for any sunlight as the world grew dark.
Today the upper boughs are ours, exposed,
the longest shadows our own longer shadows.

Crocus and bluebell clustered round the base,
shade-born like us and sprung up overnight,
were our close intimates in earlier years.
Now we commune with the sun, moon and stars,
inhale the oxygen and hoard the light
before the next storm devastates the place.

Sand

'Be sand, not oil, in the gears.'
Spend your remaining years
dodging the mean machine.
Ignore the online scene;
be like the shifting sand,
the dark volcanic kind
and the white powdery sort
of a wide western strand
or a fashionable resort.
Pour sand without stint
in complex systems meant
to make the world go round
at an increasing pace,
then listen for the sound
of engines seizing up
and shuddering to a stop.
In the ensuing peace
induced by gritty grease
we hear silence sing
clearer than anything;
then birdsong, falling rain
on window sill and drain,
a mumble where waves grind
the rocks and cliffs to sand.

Open Air

Where have they gone
who frightened everyone
with their exciting talk of revolution?

They mostly came
to terms and, growing tame,
chose gainful media or the property game.

Some who dreamed of
the obvious alternative,
a different set-up based on peace and love,

flinch from voices,
from forceful purposes,
and hide in fear with their obscure psychoses —

or so we say
in our complacent way,
not having heard from them in many a day.

In fact they're wild
with joy out in the cold,
no further nonsense from the twittering world,

since they prefer,
like us, the open air,
nothing inimical to interfere

with an ideal
relation to the real
unmediated by the quantifiable.

They (we) resort
to slow, organic thought,
having been agoraphobic from the start;

and we survive
not in the urban hive
but far away, in touch with wind and wave,

with earth and sky,
blithely untroubled by
the clamour of switched-on society —

or so we like
to imagine as we take
a drink at rush hour after our quiet work

while from the trees
creaking in a sea breeze
the crows invigilate with watchful eyes.

Around the Town

Not even his medication can restrain
Stephen, the local schizo, who calls out
quietly to the tourists, 'Why don't you lot
go home?', and to the guides, 'Shut the fuck up!'
The man's a menace; when will he ever stop?
Often you see him standing in the rain

grinning, his pale gaze on the anoraks,
those credulous, time-serving, online folks
with their smart cameras, who were never much
to his liking. Now he stares with undivided
scorn at the brisk intrusion as if such
people are dangerous and best avoided.

Not dangerous himself but best ignored
since life is short, he shows more interest
in the boats knocking next the Harbour Board,
quick ripples flickering along their sides,
and in the mysterious darklight of clouds
than in whatever rouses his distrust.

A blithe ninny, not a care in the world,
he lives in an alternative one unspoiled
by harsh reality, like the traditional clown,
the licensed fool absolved from everything;
boyish and spare, he romps around the town
with a ukulele, looking inclined to sing.

I've been observing him for many a year.
Though shining with the glow of eternal youth
he must be anxious lest the life out here
break into the studio of private myth
where he controls the strange activities
of his dream figures, their curious lives —

since, as director, he gets to rewrite
the script and give himself the best part.
Auteur, brother, I know how these things work
except I call it poetry. We should talk;
and if we do, who knows, you might impart
the secret of your own peculiar art?

Among the Rocks

Not even holidaymakers really bother
Joseph the beachcomber, who spends his days
sitting among the rocks and the rock pools
absorbed in his own thoughts, his own schedules,
like a *bōdhisāttva* or a Desert Father
for whom this life is only a glum phase.

A retired trawlerman or a long-term
invalid, though he *looks* strong enough,
he fills a plastic bag with dribs and drabs,
flotsam and jetsam — driftwood, bottles, crabs —
then, with the day's work done, recycles home
at twilight to his own mysterious gaff,

a bungalow he shares with his two brothers,
the three of them in there like grumpy dwarves.
Bundled up in oilskins and woolly scarves,
life on the beach is now his daily habit;
unsociable, quite oblivious of others,
he has the intent air of a busy Hobbit.

Summer and winter it's the same except
the scarves come off in spring when butterflies
flutter above the dunes. Seagulls inspect
his lunch box, hovering, but keep their distance
noting perhaps, like us, the glowering eyes,
the harsh brows bespeaking an existence

long alienated from the affective life.
People are a nuisance since everyone's
for ever up to some sort of mischief
with their developments and innovations.
Better the rough solitude of the rocks
where you can keep clear of the other folks

and watch the water, dozing at odd times
out of the wind. He's probably down there now
while the long day exhales and a ship chimes —
coldly at peace as the sun dips below
the Old Head and his own head registers
a silent broadband of the moon and stars.

Algae

If in any country a forest was destroyed, I do not believe so many species would perish as would, here, from destruction of the kelp.

— Charles Darwin

I WRACK

There came an era when steam first
started condensing into mist
and cloud, when the first rains broke
roaring on sedimentary rock;
when hot streams of detritus ran
and the first signs of growth began.

The earliest wrack goes that far back,
or nearly, to when sunlight struck
into those underwater caves
hidden away beneath the waves;
and there it prospers, forming now
forests where secret species grow.

Once in a while, on quiet days
after tempestuous nights, it lies
up, flea-infested, on the strand
dripping, or blown dry by wind,
squeaky and witch-brown in the sun
until the next tide takes it down;

and rarely, when a cyclone strikes,
wrack will howl above the rocks,
a wild insurgency let fly
and throwing shapes against the sky
to mock our easy common sense
and shock our breezy confidence.

2 DULSE

The overpowering stench of algae
gives rise to an old nostalgia.
Thinking of the red dulse we knew
at seaside places years ago,
its leafy weave and dusky taste,
I'm back there on the Antrim coast.

Brodsky describes how a first whiff
of dulse transported him as if
to the cold winters of his youth;
and further back, to the salt breath
of our dark origins amid
slow-to-develop squirts and squid.

If dreams reveal not just the real
biography of a single soul
but the whole history of the race,
even my dulse dream has its place —
recording, as it does, a time
when we had scarcely quit the slime.

Dulse and the like you can pick up
from beaches or a seaside shop.
Today it tastes the same as in
the spring of nineteen forty-nine
and even, who knows, the distant age
before our own crowd took the stage.

3 KELP

Now they're cutting away the kelp
on an industrial scale; so help
save the seaweeds in Bantry Bay!
Why do they want it, by the way?
To make new medicines of course;
but the mermaid and the water horse,

the kelpie, up to their thrashing hips
in those live, iodine-rich depths,
will not be pleased. Maggie Dirrane
from Bob Flaherty's *Man of Aran*,
with a big load of kelp and wrack
stacked like turf on her broad back

to fertilize the spuds and such
in her resourceful garden patch,
will not be happy; shrimp and prawn
will die without it, and the one
crab left out on a starlit shore
will find no refuge any more.

Even as I write this I can hear
a chainsaw cough and start to clear
the hillside of its remaining trees
for building on. Don't do it, please!
Just let the old birch and hazel be,
and the cloud forests of the sea.

Spuds in Space

*Remains this crumbling and savoury lump — which lends itself
less to subsistence, though this comes first, than to philosophizing.*
— Francis Ponge, 'La pomme de terre',
tr. John Montague

If the epic epoch of space exploration
still lies ahead, no doubt the star-wars crowd
will excavate rare minerals on the moon
and, if they don't screw up, quite probably
investigate those curious knobbly
rocks, potato-shaped, beyond Neptune —
another corner where life started out,
promoted by a chance irradiation.

Spuds in space! But don't we *live* in space
with our own spuds, our venerable life-source?
Rice and quinoa work for us too of course
but Paddy's spud has pride of place —
perhaps because its surface is like ours
in texture, the peculiar bumps, the eyes;
perhaps because it was our best resource,
that and poached salmon, in pre-Famine days.

Open it up and the moist interior breathes
a fresh scent of the earth, of rain and leaves,
pristine and glistening despite the mud
and stony soil stuck to the outer spud.
Sniff the blue headlands of July
in the firm body. Chipped and fried, it goes
with salt and vinegar to satisfy
old-fashioned drinkers after the pubs close;

boiled, baked or mashed, it is the very stuff
of life itself, and when we've had enough
we're left with a clean plate and bits of skin.

Now we've eaten earth, consumed the earth;
for this our 'crumbling lump' in space,
so savoury, can't save itself from us
with our voracious jaws and ravenous teeth.
What remains goes into the compost bin.

Take a late walk then on a coastal path
as light dies in the evening, August light
rich and exhausted, little cloud or wind —
ripening fruit and quiet, abundant growth
on the south-facing headlands. Never mind
the bare horizon and depleted beach;
look to the twinkling farms, starlit
potato fields as far as the eye can reach.

Nacht und Träume

Enchanted night, you're fading hence
and faintly too the dreams depart
as the pale moonlight you dispense
lies lightly on the human heart —
dreams that pierce us with delight
so we exclaim in this new dawn:
'Come back again, enchanted night;
delightful dreams, come back again!'

Schubert, you should be living yet
to finish that symphonic score.
Meanwhile we have the Trout Quintet,
the *Winterreise* and much more,
for you wrote fast to fill with love
the night-time skies' acoustic void
in the short time you had to live
before your final winter ride.

Bring back the old rosemantic dreams
such as were popular in those years,
cool and sweet as mountain streams,
clear and sincere as rueful tears,
the water music swans would sing
at evening; these the final work
of your own quiet *Sturm und Drang*,
each song a swan song from the dark.

Kilcash

The air blew warm that summer morning
when we drove over to Slievenamon,
the ruined tower house and environs
dozing at peace there in the sun.
The old church with its Romanesque
door looked inviting, but the tower
for some reason (we didn't ask)
was closed to the casual visitor.

No one goes up there now except
lovers, and locals from the modest
Georgian outbuildings, who've kept
the place unchanged from when the last
Butlers and Brownes departed thence
first having sold the hazel woods
for timber — common practice once —
or so the familiar song records.

You can just picture it as it was
in the old times, although these here
are old times too, these are the days
before the real world with its severe
demands insists on an income stream,
a seasonal influx of tourist cash
to the romantic history dream
you still embody for us, Kilcash.

A True Note

i.m. Ciaran Carson, obiit 6/10/19

Candlelight in Portstewart,
forty-odd years ago now,
and your tin whistle starts
the tots jigging as though
instinctively they know
just what to dance and how.

Astonishing, as if you'd
drawn from the atmosphere
the mysteries circling there,
spirits of field and cliff.
Oh, everything had soured
that wasn't already off,

but your fierce rhapsody
floated above Belfast like
an archangel in the sky
staring down from a cloud
at iron, rope, red brick,
factory and back yard

through smoky rain, dropping
tears of infinite grief
and promising some relief;
your skipping, fluent song
tripped from a nimble tongue
until the music stopped.

Still life goes on. Out there
pebbles 'clock' on the shore,
discordant details thrive
in the chaos where we live

and a true note can be heard:
the voice of a blackbird,

descendant of the bird
noted in marginal ink
by a ninth-century monk
transcribing on goatskin
our formal rubric: 'In
the beginning was the Word' . . .

b/w

1 BRIGHTON ROCK

The shelter on the promenade survives
where the vile boy suborned credulous Rose.
The teashop is still open where he proposed
though the West Pier has sunk beneath the waves
with its 'authentic tang of fish and chips'
in vinegar and newsprint . . . The Old Ship
where Ida reigned is thriving. Her revenge:
while the protection mob from the racecourse
howl in perpetual fire she's in the lounge
laughing, and with enough cash in her purse
for port and Guinness any sunny holiday —
big-hearted, game for a cuddle, never-say-die.

2 SUNSET BLVD.

Gloria Swanson plays one final card
while the sun sets on Sunset Boulevard.
This is her swansong, and the star system
glitters again now as the light goes west
in a last blaze of glory. Max and Joe
condone the dream she's grown addicted to
in a moving picture of peak Hollywood
(nothing thereafter will be half as good).
Joe, though soon to die in the swimming pool,
admires the old girl, really, for her brave
determination and her frantic love of
life, 'which can be strangely merciful'.

3 LA STRADA

The mighty Zampanò who bursts his chains
can't break free of his own violent nature
not even for Gelsómina, gentle creature.
She finds her consolation with the clowns
but there's no consolation for the bold
strongman when he deserts her on the road
and, self-condemned to a grim solitude,
has no alternative but to fight the world.
Sentimental, perhaps, but the heart sighs
for the poor bastard when he realizes
what he's lost by throwing his weight around
and writhes in grief on a deserted strand.

4 WILD STRAWBERRIES

Clock without hands . . . He knows his time is short
but first he travels for an honorary doctorate
to be conferred on him by the *alma mater*.
The old sunlit face shines with a secret light
reflected back from his own private dream:
a world of women and girls now lost in night,
all grouped on a jetty for a boating party
in the spring fashions of an earlier time,
their voices rippling on the quiet water —
sisters or cousins, someone's growing daughter.
Taken up by the young, he's young at last
as age returns him to the distant past.

5 À BOUT DE SOUFFLE

Belmondo, bad boy, saunters in the Champs-
Élysées and the other dangerous zones.
Enchanted as in our young days by Godard's
low-budget video world of cars and bars,
we watch it with nostalgia. This is the one
we fancied most, the one that turned us on
(Jean Seberg!) when a new wave swept aside
the formulae of the previous, safe decade.
Their flip romance continues much the same
when nightly jazz is heard in the *sixième*;
but the fond hopes of the era, once so bright,
have gone like ghosts in the new corporate light.

6 THE LOVED ONE

Gielgud hangs himself from his own springboard
while Aimée Thanatogenos, corpse cosmetician,
descended from a nymph and a Greek god,
waits on the set of an exalted vision
with the low sprinklers and white statuary
of her necropolis, an erogenous zone:
funereal silence, icebox and thermostat.
Only truly alive among the shades
and cute sarcophagi of Whispering Glades,
she is transfigured there by death and art,
toning dead faces in unquestioning faith
since art's perfection is the twin of death.

7 EFFI BRIEST

for Joachim Beug

She's scarcely more than a child and far too young
for the wife of a middle-aged provincial governor.
Innstetten tries hard in his straitlaced fashion
but it comes as no surprise when things go wrong.
What we remember, though, is the misty shore,
the dunes, the pines, the magical plantation
where a mysterious Chinese, far from home,
lies in the sandy earth of Pomerania.
Whatever about the lurid twentieth century
I quickly recognize that bleak country,
the squinting windows and harsh oversight
that always saw the world in black and white.

Saxophone

for Gerry Wrixon

Quite soon now you will play by ear
the greatest hits of yesteryear —
'Summertime', 'Stranger on the Shore',
'September Song' and many more —
if you can keep the practice up.
Some decades before rock and pop
the blue notes of a tenor sax
helped busy businessmen relax
in smoky nightclubs everywhere
from New Orleans to Soho Square.
The saxophone was in the air,
its knowing tone the sly, schmoozy
vibe of a spoilt bourgeoisie
saved from unmourned oblivion
by an ironic sense of fun
since sax lugubriously guys
its own absurd funereal noise.

  It even goes back to Berlioz
and other hipsters like Bizet
who scored for sax as long ago
as the mid nineteenth century —
and Mozart might have done so too
had sax existed in his day.
It's not hard to imagine it
featuring in *The Magic Flute*
with Papageno finding quaint
character in the instrument.
A saxophone concerto? Yeah,
why wouldn't he? Though the idea
would have outraged a court milieu
as being coarse and impudent.

The modern story of the sax
shadows political history from
the Jazz Age years of dope and sex
to D-Day and the atom bomb,
from dudes in dicky bow and tux
to sweater girls in bobby sox.
Its voice was heard above the rocks
at Newport on a summer's day
talking ecstatic peace and love;
and now it's heard at Sandy Cove,
seductive and imperious. Play
'Black Magic' or 'Amazing Grace'
and bring a smile to every face.

Real Time

What's the time now in intergalactic space?
God only knows; but the real time takes place
here on the living earth, a constant flux
since the great days of Archaeopteryx.
East wind, the gardens die, it's autumn-time;
time is the conduit and the gushing stream.

An inch of rain and a few dead leaves lie
in facing deckchairs under the night sky,
exhausted ghosts of a fraught seminar
on time, and held in time, the day, the hour
(a time-consuming exercise at best).
Absolute time, we're told, doesn't exist;

real time, the moving picture, is the thing —
those deckchairs, and the faint creak of a swing
strung up from a low branch. Nothing besides
is happening, only a present that provides
its presence to remind us that you, time,
create the context and the continuum.

Jailer, historian and philosopher, you
who keep us under constant close review
around the clock, may we not ever take,
even for a second, a reflective break,
unsupervised, to try 'eternal' themes
discredited in these existential times?

Radiance

Gym-fit to work but dream-deprived,
the early chronotypes are on the road
at furious daybreak while the longer-lived
late risers, slothful, doubtful, lie abed
until the town is freshly aired.

Touching the void — oh, years ago —
the sun burst into flames 'and there was light'
wherever it sent out its productive glow;
but surely we don't mean to abolish night
with blue-rich radiance shining bright

on field and stream without relief,
airports and sports facilities, hi-tech premises,
white wastes of the contemporary life.
Where now is the shadowy anamnesis
with its mysterious promises?

Darken our blinding light a bit
and turn the volume down so we can hear
ourselves thinking, if we've a taste for thought;
even now the obscure silences might survive
where an original thought can thrive.

St Cecilia's Day

for Paul Simon

Cecilia, you can break the heart
and shake the confidence daily. On my knees
inside your elegant church in bright Trastevere,
I listened to the organ, charmed by every
chord and grace note, each archaic wheeze
of pipe and keyboard. Your high art,

composed of air and rapture, cries
to heaven for intervention with a tremor
caught from the heavens; as in the Madeleine once
hearing the organ music of Saint-Saëns,
the great third symphony in C minor,
I felt transported to the skies.

A child of solitude, and in serious
recognition of your consoling sound,
please may I dedicate this one to you, Paul,
voice of an age, and that inspiring girl
Cecilia patron of music, organist, blind
interpreter of the turning spheres.

St Lucy's Day

Lucy, pre-Christmas panic throngs
the shopping districts; unrelieved rush hours,
consuming market towns and cities, blaze
and blare in the longer nights and shorter days
this season of imaginary snow showers
and commonplace commercial songs.

A crow sits out of it, apart
on a high wire, unruffled, sure in its bones
of a new world, *i.e.* 'at the next spring',
and snaps a flea from under a raised wing.
Soon enough now the January rains
and then the most exciting part

when your light, Lucy, starts to stretch
its glow on the exhausted planet. Signs
are there already, thanks to the climate thing,
that a new life will flourish when you bring
reviving colour where the last ice shines,
if ice remains, on pond and ditch.

Smoky Quartz

Thanks for the present; everything will be grand
now that I have this dark crystal at hand
to ground me with its 'strong link to the earth'.
Promising resolve and equanimity both
with its positive vibe and spiritual energy,
it works to relieve anxiety and lethargy,
helps heart and nerves, the whole constitution,
promoting tolerance and concentration.

It's a mysterious thing, transparent and opaque
like life, with faint patches of yellow light
moving around, though mostly it's black smoke
as if from buses burning at a riot,
a crippled oil rig or the world at night.

Though never used in the old crystal sets
it is its own radio and radiates
creative waves between the earth and ether,
soul and material substance. I hold it tight
in the left hand to activate the right.

An Old Theme

I shall die in due course on a day of rain.
Not in the last bed by the exit, please,
with a loud sitcom on the gogglebox
but in an armchair at the twilight hour
reading something favoured by old crocks:
gossip, philosophy, maybe Schopenhauer
(the bit where he says nature doesn't care
about individuals, only about the species).
Off I'll go to the glue factory then.

I shall die soon enough on a windy night
not quietly but furious at the outrage,
kicking and screaming as the lights go out.
Never mind; contributing my own calcium
to the world soup with rosemary, sage
and thyme, I will have time to come
to terms with the elemental afterlife —
grimly, of course, if not without relief.

We shall meet again by the shore at high tide
swimming together noisily for a minute
or know each other in a thick cloud
of dust at a bus stop before dispersing —
flecks and specks of that vast entity
'the seminal substance of the universe':
new lives, the range of options infinite.

Xanadu

North of Shangdu did Kubla Khan
a fine pavilion proudly raise
of cane transported from Hunan.
Lightweight considering its size
it was a *seasonal* pleasure dome,
not the grand palace we presume,
and in the winter taken down.
The real palace was in the town,
a quiet spot far from the haze
of hot Dadu — Beijing as is —
a cool retreat up in the hills,
no sea for two hundred miles.
Drowsing among his travel books
a poet pictured the whole box
of tricks, the curious scene set
by the sea cliffs in Somerset,
romantic chasm and bouncing rocks
(those intimations of wild sex)
an obvious topographic fit.
'Ancestral voices' was a guess
but the Chinese did wreck the place.
Now there are lots of Xanadus
with marble pools and private zoos
like the best known, if not the first,
inspired by the news mogul Hearst.

Shangdu's now an industrial zone
but the old Xanadu lives on —
a lively fantasy, at least,
in the mindscape of many a one
together with the enchanted *bonne
vaux* of Restif de la Bretonne,
the cloudy realms and Tír na nÓgs
beloved of the great mystagogues
where we abide by other laws

than those of known reality, those
that govern worldly purposes.

    Once in a while a voice is heard
broadcasting the subversive word
from a daydream or opium trance
as domes arise and boulders dance:
some visionary is with us yet,
a cryptic soul who can't forget
the sacred river, caves of ice!
Weave a circle round her thrice.

Bruges-la-Morte

1

Snuff out the candles and turn up the light;
this place could do with a bit of fun tonight —
a wicked rave, say, on a religious theme.
We've got to forget about the bad old days
when, with the sea subtracted, Bruges was dead,
nothing but *béguinages* and idle quays,
canals and churches, fog and drizzle spread
like a fine net retaining a lost dream.

2

But we've no wish to reconstruct a quaint
heaven from the belfries, from the swans below
the bridges, the damp brickwork and the faint
groan of a distant foghorn, have we now?
Besides, with the waters rising, chances are
this will become a thriving port once more,
no time for convents and their angel wings,
their thoughts on vague, unquantifiable things.

To 'Young Werther'

(Goethe)

Once more you venture forth, lamented shade,
into the light of day, encountering me
quite amicably in a fresh-flowering glade
as if you lived again in your lost youth
when evening dew refreshed us both
and after our long hours of industry
sunset enchanted us with a last gleam.
Your choice was to resign, mine to persist;
you haven't missed much in the interim.
A life on earth seems like a happy destiny,

the day so glorious and the night so vast;
but, planted in this paradisal place,
we've hardly even started to embrace
the sun when instinct, in perverse contrast,
rouses at once a strange antipathy
now to ourselves, now to the world we see,
and neither fits the other as it might.
It's dark outside despite the inner light
and a fair prospect hides from a grim gaze;
it's there at hand and we don't realize.

We think we've found it when a woman's form
bewitches us with its particular charm.
A young man, happy as a child in spring,
steps out like very spring itself, amazed,
enraptured: who has done this thing?
He looks about him and the world is his;
an urgent impulse draws him on.
Nothing constrains him, neither hedge nor door;
like a bird skimming a forest, there
he hovers, circling around the loved one

while from the clear air he will soon disown
he seeks the loving glance that tames his heart.
But, warned too soon, perhaps too late, his flight
he knows is baffled and himself ensnared.
Parting is hard and again twice as hard;
years are requited in a single look
but a harsh separation marks the end.
You smile, rightly and ruefully, old friend,
since your conclusion made you known
when we honoured your sad history in a book.

Those whom you left behind for better or worse
tread once again the labyrinthine course
of human love, since there remains for them
the always troubling and unknown future —
death at the end of it. How pure
and sure it sounds when poets sing
to cheat the death these dramas bring!
Caught in such agonies, ourselves to blame
for mad romance, may it be given to us
to speak true of the trials we have to face.

Art poétique

(Verlaine)

The music is the important thing.
Opt for the odd, the singular,
the faint, the soluble in air,
no rhetoric and no posturing.

Take note, it's absolutely fine
to sound a bit ambiguous;
best is a grey, indefinite verse
where the exact and vague combine —

behind the veil a twinkling eye,
vibration of the noonday light,
a violet star concourse, bright
in an exhausted autumn sky.

Not primary colour but nuance,
nuance alone that can unite
dream to dream and horn to flute,
informs all such experience.

Resist the lure of biting 'wit',
the glib reductionism, the cheap
sarcasm at which angels weep.
Avoid the nasty taste of it.

Take eloquence and wring its neck
and, while we're at it, it's high time
to be more circumspect with rhyme.
If not, it soon dictates the work.

The damage it has done already!
What daft idiot, deaf to tone,

forged from tin this specious coin
that rings so thin to everybody?

Music and yet more music, please!
May your own song be something light
we hear soaring, a soul in flight
to other loves and other skies.

May it presage the greater future
borne on a brisk morning wind
bestowing scents of thyme and mint.
The rest is only literature.

Down in the Woods

(Verlaine)

Some, like the innocent and the neurasthenic,
find in the woods only a languorous charm,
fresh breezes, warm scents. Good luck to them.
Others, dreamers, are seized with vague panic.

Good luck to them! I, nervous and aghast,
racked by a strange, insistent guilt complex,
tremble here like a faintheart who expects
a trap, perhaps an encounter with a ghost.

These great boughs, like sea waves never still,
with their dark silences and even darker
shadows — a sad and sinister décor —
inspire fears both profound and risible.

Worst is summer dusk when a fiery sky
merges in the grey-blue of mists its range
of blood hues while a distant angelus
rings out like the echo of a plaintive cry.

Wind rises hot, strong; wild convulsions race
crazily through the increasingly opaque
density of the oaks until, grown weak,
they escape like exhalations into space.

Night hovers, an owl flies, and you think back
to grim rumours warning of awful things.
Below a thicket there, *there*, hidden springs
chuckle like killers lying in wait to strike.

After Swift

You used to wish you had a decent
income to cover moderate rent,
a nice flat with some extra space,
gardens to sit out on warm days,
sea views and a private wood
somewhere in the neighbourhood.
These you now have, to your relief,
with no desire for city life —
the traffic chaos, the grim crowd,
'pedestrian precincts' and the loud
rock music heard on every side.
Unlike *Swift* you'd take no part
in politics, that wicked sport.
You've got to watch them even so:
the frank venality shows through
in every aspect of existence
even though you keep your distance.
Caught up in a hectic trance
where we think only of finance,
you'd be condoning an inflationary
set-up you can't take seriously;
you'd find yourself, as in the past,
a truculent, bewildered guest
at launch parties, art openings,
poetry nights and other things
where folks demand continually
'Please can you sign a book for me'
and some, aware of your chagrin,
look on with an ironic grin.

Bailey who gives me bad reviews
seems to believe I don't mind those
and *Shelbourne*, an inimical force,
comes on like an old pal of course.

These, from conventional ambition,
neck, and political discretion,
thrive in a slick society
frightened of contrariety.
Knocking the market, placing blame
where it belongs, is not for them,
nor for them either the fond dream
of a subversive future when
'financial services' break down.
Meanwhile in the high-rising town
cars, cash and competition.

    Just so, in such wasteful hours
I'd squander my declining powers,
for ever thinking of this sober
work table above the harbour.
Here in my quiet inglenook
I doze or read a serious book
ignoring, in reflective slowth,
the world of economic growth.

Dust

You keep on saying it's time to dust
the dusty table, chairs and shelves.
Right, go ahead then if you must,
they're not about to dust themselves;
but leave my writing desk alone!
It doesn't shine as once it shone
but that's no reason to upset
the careful chaos, please, not yet:
there's some more typing to be done
before I hang my sneakers up.
I grant you, now, that table top
is getting a bit much: I could
inscribe my name there on the wood
with a schoolboyish finger. Oh
and look, the carpet, that could do
with a good hoovering from you
while I, too busy to pay heed,
sit in another room and read.

It's not the dust here but the ash
I drop with nonchalant panache
scribbling and smoking, both at once.
'Ashes to ashes, dust to dust' —
this is the mortal circumstance
waiting for us, like moth and rust.
Artistic aims pursued since youth
can taste like ashes in the mouth
when other things are factored in:
the death of loved ones, too much gin;
neglect, too late now to repair,
and high ideals that never were.

No, dust and ashes, wipe them off!
We can't remove them fast enough.

The lovely cobwebs hung with flies,
grave and mysterious in our eyes,
superfluous hair and bits of skin —
consign them to the litter bin
and let's have a new-shining space
innocent of the past, to face
another, sunnier summertime
confidently and free from shame.

   The dust, though, what becomes of it?
Does it disperse as being unfit
for human purpose? Yes and no.
It blows away like sand or snow
but then regroups and merges with
the live components of the earth.
See that block of apartments? Dust.
Manhattan Equity and Trust?
Dust; and to dust all these return.
It's from the dust that we were born.

Washing Up

You do the gastronomy; I wash up
and rinse under a running tap.
I like it, on the whole. It gives
me time to think about our lives
here at the edge, no, at the *eye*
of real existence, wind and sky
working together to define
the limits of our own domain.
There's so much washing up to do
on the degraded planet now —
oceans and forests, oily sands,
our filthy-lucrative demands
on the resources of this place
and soon, perhaps, of outer space.
Beyond the window a bright star
notes my performance from afar,
twinkling to find a widower
engaged on a domestic chore —
a relic of pre-digital times,
fond of anachronistic rhymes,
in flight from the new *politique*
of induced squalor and high tech
washed up on a deserted beach
grumpy, contrarian, out of reach.

I stand here at the kitchen sink
watching the soap bubbles blink . . .
No, here at the sink I stand
with a wet drying-cloth in hand
dreaming, not of that caricature
an automatic dishwasher

but of an even simpler life
untouched by electronic stuff.
The best of miracles rely
on the old, known reality —
pines where the woodpigeons live,
wild garlic growing in the drive,
the nightly fun of wiping dry
dishes and bowls and cutlery.

Washing up here along this shore
us urban exiles can be sure
of a real world where fauna thrive
and precious habitats survive;
where swifts back from Rwanda find,
unchanged, the nests they left behind
and hungry gulls remain content
with their own fishy nourishment.
However much we wish her ill
nature as such is hard to kill:
the more insistent our demands
the more severely she responds
by turning up the heat again
so we too register the pain.
Golfers in helicopters fly
here, dropping daily from the sky,
and surfers surf who might prefer
not to be here but in Hawaii —
but these are just technology
playing its games with sea and air.

Knowing our own place, I infer
from my perspective as *plongeur*,
in the whole turbulent shebang,
the universe and everything,

is the one miracle that wins
out over a rake of sins.
It might be going too far to say
life is worth living anyway
for the naive and unprepared
despite the violence endured
or the despondent migrant crowds
out on the road like drifting clouds:
what do *we* know in our resigned
enclosure, sheltered from the wind?
But don't we cherish, all the same,
our long-sought equilibrium?

I stack the plates with diligence,
glad to have been of use for once,
and step outside to watch the sea
washing up in the estuary.

Another Cold Spring

Another cold spring —
the same as last year,
the previous year also,
a late storm papering
the daffodils with snow
and leaving the sky clear.

We can't depend upon
the meteorology from one
month to the next, the seasonal
graph of established weather
having been since revised
or scrapped altogether;

but when could we ever?
We know how to make do
with what the skies bestow;
hence the bluff stoicism,
routine if you prefer,
built into the system.

Another cold spring, though,
audible day and night
beneath a hanging bough,
bursts from the undergrowth,
once a monastic site
or anchoritic bower.

The water is spring-clean,
freezing to hand and mouth
straight from the dark earth,
fresh from an open field,
undoctored, undefiled,
lime-filtered, crystalline.

It has been flowing there
for ages out of mind,
this secretive, demure
whisper in the wind,
a tiny field of force
and an unfailing source

of what, the numinous?
Perhaps the 'spiritual'
if the old word retain
some of its former use,
analogous to the virtual
plainsong of a drain.

Tree-shaded from the sun
it stays icy cold when
air temperatures improve,
refusing to submit
anything of its nature
to the hot world above —

as if to say, 'This slight
outpouring isn't meant
for your enlightenment
but for my own delight;
still, if it tastes right,
take of it what you want.'

Byron to Moore

(Palazzo Mocenigo, 4 March 1820)

I write again while the fit's on me, Tom,
in hopes a busy man like you can come
and join us in the perpetual *Bacchanal*
at our damp 'palace' on the Grand Canal
if only for a month. It's not that I'm
lonely exactly, since I spend my time
gaily with dark-eyed beauties and a pack
given to gaming, wine and Armagnac
when not riding and swimming at the Lido,
perchance *gondoling* with a pretty widow;
but I want to hear what's going on these days
in the cold land of Pitts and Castlereaghs.
When my own thoughts turn upon liberty
I dream of Greece, perhaps Armenia, free
of brutal empire and the imperial trash.
Everything, in the end, comes down to *cash*;
the rogues and rascals who would own the earth
will never tire. We give them 'a wide berth'
but their insistent purposes confine
the generous inclinations, yours and mine.
      I notice the d—n'd *Quarterly Review*
is out again with its constricted view
of modern verse; and this is just the start,
believe me. I don't mind, for my own part,
but I care about your future reputation.
Some bright spark of the younger generation
will denigrate the *Melodies*, or will try:
genius and fame always incur hostility.
Someone will say you make a music-box
of the wild harp, but never mind such folks:
think of the thousands who will keep your line
a-singing, and the lamp lit at your shrine.

Sure in your place as Erin's national Bard,
you need have no real fears in that regard.
A hundred years from now, when we're both dead,
your lovely *Lalla Rookh* will still be read
and your fine songs sung to the *piano-forte*
wherever friends make up an evening party
or your compatriots convene to mourn
the sad state of the Isle where you were born.
    Do tear yourself away from th'other guests,
the manly compliments and sighing breasts.
The 'most serene repub.' awaits, with me,
your imminent descent.

Yrs. ever, — B.

A Line of Moore

' . . . And all but he departed.' Now the great
figures have gone, the rest of us await
the extinction of the species at long last.
Our work started out in the distant past,
taking its origins from the dawn of time;
the present product, though, is looking dim
and as for the *coming* times, who can be sure?
The quick lights sparkle and as soon expire
as if deprived of serious themes. I blame
our own predisposition to play the game,
confused reluctance to take on the task
of speaking truth to power. Averse to risk,
we always tended to avoid criticism
of what kills even our own value system
like the explosive growth of high finance
directing thought, with nothing left to chance:
long gone the heroic poets who would write
out of conviction and tormented insight
into the workings of the world and raise
cracked voices amid the conventional noise.
Now, watching friends begin their afterlives,
contemporaries around me fall like leaves,
I fear for the future relevance of the art.
Who will there be to banish from the state
when the remaining singers sing along
to the Platonic 'perfect harmony' song
beloved of the huge private enterprises?
Wary of these, even as they hand out prizes,
I walk a silent hall with the lights off
and bay leaves wrinkling on a tablecloth.
    This is the morning after. Soon the dry
cleaners will come to clear the plates away
leaving an empty space for the next lot,
sales representatives as like as not;

but everything has gone beyond satire
what with the global 'economic satur-
ation' remarked by Arendt years ago
and now complete from Maui to Mayo
or almost. The resistance can be found
among those recusants who stand their ground
against the invaders and the insistent sort
spreading poison even to the last resort.
   Some of the fallen leaves could be a pain
and yet I grieve that they won't come again
throwing the snide asides and glancing blows
with which we kept each other on our toes.
So life is more relaxed but, strange to say,
I miss the cut and thrust of an earlier day,
the rough-and-tumble signifying serious
fear of developments in the public sphere.
No fear today, few voices to defy
consensus as we face the next catastrophe.
O young inheritors, it's time to fight
the long discredited armies of the night!

Chekhov at the Grove

It wouldn't do for crowd scenes — *Cyrano*,
Brook's *Māhabhārata, Macbeth* — or Noh;
but it's fine for a sketch, an intimate revue
or a pair of one-act comedies like these two
starting this evening, since the theatre
is a converted garage cleared of dust,
a tight space the stage makes even tighter.
It can seat only fifty or so at most.

We're putting on *The Bear* and *The Proposal*,
the same three players in a double bill
and the same simple set: a living room,
table and chairs, old sepia photos visible,
the place an immersive *living room* of actors
crowding into the tiny auditorium
with a wound-up participatory buzz —
themselves a local list of characters.

Private theatricals? Oh yes, no doubt,
but Cal Duggan's production benefits from
her practical experience of the form,
the easy expertise she brings to it.
Spectators mob the place, *le tout* Kinsale,
and Olga on the accordion plays them in.
Iliena and her servant Luke begin
and Smirnov's showing up in a short while.

It was *The Bear* that made his name
and *The Proposal* brought him fame;
a few years later *The Seagull*
confirmed him as the life and soul
of the new drama, and in time
the snobby Brits adopted him,
delighted with the weary tone
of country houses like their own.

During the short interval
we mingle on the gravel
by magical starlight,
the same stars as shone
on the Crimean shore
before the first world war,
the October Revolution
and subsequent confusion.
Do we relive tonight
a vanished age of Tsars?
No, for even the stars
lighting the strange scene
differ from how they were
in those fantastic years.

Only the spirit will survive
this constant flux of atoms when
the ancient earth returns to dust;
there will be no one left alive,
no actors or spectators then
and the playtext of history lost.
So says young Trepliov, but we
don't need to take him seriously.

Natasha and Ivan are there,
she in an apron, he in tails
the better to propose to her.
His shaky resolution fails
(everything of importance failed
in that ferocious neverland
except in the artistic field);
and yet it works out in the end.

He'd seen the lower depths, the convicts chained
in Sakhalin; but that wasn't the end
of the long story, since he kept alive
always the bright hope of an alternative.
His own doctor, the playwright knew already
the fatal virus active in the body
like a slow thermal image hard at work
in a mysterious forest after dark.

Great thing about a miniature proscenium,
you can't be taken in: it's only some
neighbours pretending on a tiny stage
set up for four nights in an old garage.
Gripping, though, and the excitement lies
not in the simple action of the plays
but in the spectacle of friends recast
into dramatic attitudes at last

acting out things they've their own knowledge of,
panic and rage, feigned sorrow, dizzy love.
They're only amateurs, but even so
we can embody only what we know.
The beauty of it lies in their generous
giving of themselves to the night and us;
for this is real drama, not a charade,
and the cast join us for a drink outside.

Quarantine

The privileged crowd in the *Decameron*,
avoiding plague in town, beguiled the days
recounting stories scurrilous and profane;
but we can't amuse ourselves like these
since virtual quarantine is in force
against the dreaded virus. Here we sit,
each of us in seclusion, writing verse
and reconciled to an indefinite wait.

What started it, some rogue bacterium
indignant at our plant-genetic drive?
Some botched experiment, some initiative
dreamt up by a special bio-ops dream team?
Pneumonic flu is here and we have to cope
but there's no need to abandon hope
for this presages, maybe, a new age
averse to conflict and financial rage.

It's silver-lining time now that the vague
threat represented by the *tourist* plague
recedes and the place is dozing once again
in its narcotic haze of drizzling rain
with much-reduced commerce and circumstance
and even a bit of peace for once.
Bad news, though, from abroad: so many
stricken, and buried with scant ceremony

as in pre-modern times, as in *La Peste.*
Buried disease irrupts out of the past:
'Dormant for years in linen and furniture',
it sends its rats to die in the open air.
Some human agent? Nature getting back
at human agency? An ambulance
goes wailing up the road as a stoic
shopper emerges into the eerie silence.

Confined to quarters because coughs, sneezes
and even shared spaces spread diseases,
we turn to Exodus and *The Seventh Seal*,
to Nashe and book six of Lucretius:
'Bad germs invade the atmosphere
so we pick up infection as we inhale.'
A shrill wind whistles above the houses;
a briny stench blows from the roaring shore.

A Fox in Grafton St.

Broad daylight, and on weed-grown cobblestones
deserted by the pedestrian population
a fox hunts for discarded edibles —
fried chips, spare ribs or chicken bones;
but everywhere from Bewley's to McDonald's
is shut and shuttered for the duration.

Sam's a celebrity fox, an online hero
briefly promoted to the infosphere,
his bold image shared by a world of folks
anxious, like him, for sustenance. Can a fox
not do its solitary, unorthodox
research without some human interference?

Desperate now, he quarters an empty strip
sniffing at every drain and rubbish tip.
This should be a great time for foxes
but there are no scraps, no pizza boxes
stuffing the bins so they overflow.
(The young aren't going there right now.)

He'd be far better off where he belongs,
out in the country with its hens and ducks,
rabbits, fieldmice and other tasty things.
No doubt he's puzzled since the very *vox
pop* barely whispers and the electric songs
are silent; but, in a shameful paradox,

there reigns a shocked euphoria during this
short respite, this enforced parenthesis.
We're back in the days before we declared war
on the last outposts of resilient nature —
even, perhaps, in some oblique future
only dreamers ever dreamt before.

Around the House

The armchair where I sit
faces the west window.
Directly on my right
a cold hearth, never lit,
the shelf above it lined
with cards of every kind;
a heater, and the same
armchair for *Madame*
with a bookcase behind
and model planes on top;
knick-knacks and local art
of the superior sort;
folding doors, a step up
into the kitchen; then,
still circling round
the living room, another
bookcase, an old chest
of drawers, until at last
the front door, facing east,
a high window to gather
sunlight and look down
at the Scilly side of town;
desk, paper, typewriter,
Tipp-Ex, Pritt and pen
and back where we began.

    Now that you've your own
house, studio and so on
your partner sleeps alone
in the big double bed,
lays down his funny head
like an old child in its cot,
dead to the world if not
quite altogether dead.

The springs remember many
a more convivial night;
there one of your 'Horizons'
hangs, a living presence,
a two-tone colour harmony
much like the one we share,
and there too is your nude
back-portrait by Boucher
in tempting plenitude:
what would your father say?
But I'm no use today,
after the prostate op,
and bed is for rehearsing
the song the angels sing
since time must have a stop.
I do like waking up
to see the earth made new
in this mild atmosphere,
knowing I'm still alive
and thinking of the few
things to be done a poor
codger can still achieve.

   White tile, a proper *bath*,
a brush for rotten teeth,
bay rum for the skull
and a whole cupboardful
of medicines and creams:
the bathroom of your dreams.
Once lazy about hygiene,
we now want to be clean,
a regular clean-up
with fancy herbal soap
to please fastidious friends.

Wash the hands, wash the hands!
Not easy to imagine
the grime of earlier times,
the widespread body odour
under the talcum powder,
important persons even
stinking to high heaven:
much more advanced to have
a whiff of aftershave,
detergent or cologne.
Meanwhile the privy scum
goes down the drain, down
into the earth to grow
daisies in the meadow.

    Daisy-fresh, we come
out of the clearing steam
to face the day ahead:
post if there's any post,
yoghurt, fruit and toast —
then, lightly breakfasted,
on with the old oilskin;
the short walk into town.

Oedipus at Colonus

It's down to me alone. I was ashamed
but thankful and relieved to hear the damned
plague lifted at last and stricken Thebes
prospered again as formerly. It required
my own self-exile among neighbouring tribes,
some hostile, years of wandering and a hard
old age to expiate my innocent crimes.
I always did suspect the truth of course.
As plague persisted, as reports grew worse
and the place stank of corpses, there were times
I thought of giving voice to my worst fears;
then the light dawned and everything was known.
No light now, only thoughts of the plague years
and dead Jocasta, wife to her own son.
I rest on my fortuitous rock throne
staring, if I could stare, at the distant sea,
safe in a daughter's care (who wouldn't be?)
and the protection of the local god.
Death awaits us at the end of the road;
only in death are we beyond catastrophe.
Think no one happy while he's still alive;
no one is really at peace before he die
and find immunity in a tranquil grave.
Bow to the ruling principle of chance,
the lightning bolt flung from a blue sky
and now a lasting part of our inheritance.

A Quiet Day in Tangier

after Tahar Ben Jelloun

A rainstorm from the east keeps him at home
in his detached house with its flaking paint
and rotten woodwork, and exacerbates
chronic bronchitis, curse of his old age.
The few remaining cronies seldom come
to visit, since this tedious complaint,
not helped by smoking, causes violent fits
of raw coughing and misanthropic rage.

A widower, he manages for himself
or not; the few tins on the kitchen shelf
diminish slowly, for he scarcely eats.
Uninterested in the neighbours, he retreats
by preference into a magnanimous past,
the only place he feels truly at rest.
Hard work he relished, love and fatherhood,
but family doesn't suit his present mood.

Objects and furniture are a real problem —
table and radio, basin and cafetière,
the ancient sofa with its broken springs,
those conscious, knowing, oddly spiteful things
which will outlive his time by many a year.
Why can he never come to terms with them?
Choking, wheezing, trying to catch his breath,
he watches as they watch for his own death.

It's coming . . . He was never one for sport
but there's a match on in a bar nearby,
the clientèle shouting, and for a short
space he wishes he too could be there
among them, bursting with vitality,
at one with the enthusiastic crowd.

Any minute now and the lowering cloud
will clear to a fresh, rain-washed atmosphere.

It's coming, not as a seizure or a stroke
but as a vision. When the wind dies down,
the rain stops and a blinding sun comes out,
he tries a cautious venture into town;
but, intercepted in the rue Quevedo
by a young woman on a motorbike,
her lovely face familiar long ago,
he's driven off into a world of light.

Li T'ai-Po

(701-762)

He didn't drown, exactly, in the water
reaching out to seize the reflected moon
but died from double pneumonia later.
She, the effective cause of the fever,
probably wondered where he'd gone,
her most devoted and persistent lover.
Searching the earth for her Endymion,
night after night she rose and shone,
rises and shines on pond and sea,
a mysterious symbol of continuity
in the great flux and confusion.

Who can ever forget the butterfly
dreaming it was Lao Tzu, the cold tears
of the courtesan on the dewy jewel-stairs
leading down from the girls' domain
or the lone sail on the wide river
to 'heaven', where the great convene?

Diary Extract (Late T'ang)

1

Autumn we do our best creative work —
perhaps since that's when we re-dedicate
our brushes to the fine art of poetry,
perhaps because the days grow short and dark.
Making a night of day, a day of night,
we sit late at the paper and inkpot;
characters take shape by candlelight
or lamplight, while an owl hoots from a tree.

2

K'uei-chou is quiet in the morning sun.
Mists on the Yangtse soon evaporate
to leave the river clear in each direction,
vanishing where the earth and heaven meet.
Remote from the chequerboard of Ch'ang-an life,
its anxious rulers, crafty knights and rooks,
I look back with a sigh of disbelief
and give myself entirely to the books.

3

Empires, whatever their proclaimed virtues,
succumb to age, invasion, viruses,
intrigue, decadence, natural disaster,
entropy; and our own T'ang dynasty
won't last for ever. I can visualize
a distant future when we're undermined
by unknown forces, and our souls confined —
not in my lifetime or my children's, please.

4

Today I made the spiritual mistake
of thinking us serene, for it won't do
to picture it in words, much less to speak
of such a thing. Serenity doesn't know;
it's far too busy contemplating Tao
to relish its advantages and how
they coalesce. Be satisfied to remain
at peace, unbothered on the astral plane.

5

A gibbon cries and the moon casts its glow
on ivy, on a proud head humbled now
by failure in the government service,
my contributions of ill-timed advice
ignored in favour of more urgent things
like keeping the rich rich and the rest poor,
this never mentioned in the literature
or even acknowledged in committee meetings.

6

Walked in the forest: goldfinch in a bush,
hawk on a thermal, pheasants in undergrowth.
The ways are busy, families in a rush
to escape famine, pestilence or both.
Clear crystal weather, perpendicular smoke
from a few chimneys; everyone abroad
for the last sunny days, gleaners at work
in cropped fields. Saw vixen on the road.

7

Dead leaves under the door, now a first frost
puts paid to the peaches in the orchard
as war will finish off the old regime —
although for now the countryside looks most
like the ideal country in a sketch
by Wang Wei at his best, a precise dream
of the Confucian realm we love so much;
but times change, nothing is set to last.

8

Kung be damned, I've had more than my due
of *yang*'s constraint on the imagination.
If it's a choice of Li Po or Tu Fu
I choose Li Po for his superior *yin*
and his sure instinct for the longer view.
His moon-on-the-wave and similar preludes,
night-born, spring from the fresh inspiration
of an original gift. Saw bear in woods.

9

White water-curtains drop from a great height
to mist and rainbows in a gorge upstream,
for ever in transition, still the same,
like the great world itself in its orbit.
Others to east and west may take us down
with war and even 'diplomatic' force
but we shall win through in the long run;
our old ideas will triumph in due course.

10

The ancient wisdom, never quite dispersed,
shines like a rainbow in our prose and verse,
dance and philosophy. The greatest danger
comes from Tibet and ignorant warlords
with their rapacity and wild Tatar hordes.
We haven't even met the blue-eyed stranger.
If that day ever dawns it will be the worst,
though when his crude hegemony no longer (. . .)

Specimen Days

1 HART CRANE

'They know a body under the wide rain'
carries us back some ninety years or so
to the industrial zones at a tough time
of silent factories and hungry men
lining up at the unemployment bureaux
daily (*Buddy, can you spare a dime?*) —
same thing from the Bowery to Golden Gate.
Beneath the violent rage to dominate,
an earth spirit sings for those who know.
It doesn't do to be importunate though:
only after a long, considerate courtship
would the rich body yield its secrets up.

2 ELIZABETH BISHOP

A dreamy orphan, even as a fresher
you were already an acknowledged genius
with a frank innocence and simple pleasure
in a seal's gaze or the stench of gasoline,
the shores and rocky coves of Nova Scotia.
A slow riser, sensitive to cockcrow
on Cape Cod, in Key West, at Ouro Prêto
or any home, wherever home might be,
you had no home, really, except the sea.
My, those roosters did give you an earful,
wandering off however as you came to
and started in to work, 'awful but cheerful'.

3 SAMUEL MENASHE

Built from dust, from the articulate bones
of the dead generations, Jerusalem
lives not only in concrete and cut stones
but also in the fraught souls of its sons
and daughters, not as a city but as a dream;
for the real cities were the other ones
like yours on its long island, in its fridge,
where an old widow at her window ledge
watches a man 'entrenched against the snow',
a seasoned veteran still fighting through
to the bare bones of speech and finding rare
gems of particulate vision glittering there.

4 CAROLYN FORCHÉ

'The ache of some field song in Salvador'
echoes the song in every breaking heart.
A long time since the rainmakers started
bashing in their own 'back yard' door
for treasure; every life-hating dictator
had the cool patronage of the White House
in coming down hard on the indigenous
and anyone — Romero or Guevara —
crazy enough to speak for the rural poor.
But keep the liberal peace people far
from the soft borders of the sad republics:
privilege and best intentions seldom mix.

Winter Garden

(Neruda)

Winter, and slow leaves clothed
in silence and yellow
give resplendent dictation.

I'm a book of snow,
an open hand, a wide meadow,
a hopeful horizon;
I belong to the earth and its winter.

The murmur of the world rose in the branches.
The months went by, the fugitive
sky was a bowl of summer
and the driving cloud dispersed.

As if the past were back, with its childhood ivy,
I waited in grief on the balcony
for the earth to stretch its wings
over my disinhabited love.

I knew the rose would wilt,
the seasonal peach-stone sleep and increase;
I drank air until
the whole sea went dark
and the rainbow turned to ashes.

But the world lives on,
softening its interrogation,
stretching the skin of its silence.
Come from afar, I'm taciturn now,
enveloped in cold rain and bells.
To the pure death of the earth I owe
my wish to germinate and grow.

Word to the Wise

for Michael D. Higgins

La primavera caminó al mercado . . .
— Neruda, 'El Pueblo'

A Uachtaráin, as you know much better than I,
the paradigm shift on which the best rely
to save the world may be at last in sight —
distant, perhaps, but clear in a clear light
after the years of 'unreleased expectancy'.
If I may say so, your own contribution
has been a distinct credit to the nation.
(A poet, you won't mind if I invoke
poetic privilege for this kind of talk.)
What we admire most about your performance
is its high-spirited independent stance
on the inflated 'neo-liberal' programme
that makes no secret of its global scam
designed to further enrich the grisly cliques
who have the populations by their necks
as they have always had; an obvious truth.
I don't mean to put words into your mouth
but you're on record speaking for the side
of those who want an end to ecocide
and hope for a more equitable, radical,
heartening socio-economic model.
The answer, as you know yourself, is 'simple
but not easy'; to change minds for example,
to get through to the venal and the obtuse,
put manners on that shower in Leinster House,
devolve the ownership of the country to
the people of the country, not the few,
and certainly not to the invasive sort
who come to pick off what they can exploit,

leaving us to depend on the sale of drink
and fret about 'what visitors will think'.
Not easy to undo the cleverly complex
structures and expose the crude subtext
of profit frenzy some facilitate
for their own reasons; but it's not too late,
is it, to exercise here and abroad
your constitutional option to spread word
to the wise, of an old idea long overdue.
What need of a government when we have you
to stand at a night window in the Áras
and mind our tiny bit of the universe?
　　'Spring has wandered into the marketplace'
amid the loaves and doves, the bread and peace —
only a spirit as yet, though there are signs.
The driving cloud disperses, the sun shines
but not too brightly since we want to keep
some quaint obscurity, to enable sleep
and dark thought hidden from the thought police
who can detect estrangement in a trice.
(Oh yes, a conspiracy theorist, I'm quick
to note the inimical aspects of high tech.)
It's our tradition, is it not, to hide
our secret fictions from the world outside,
imagining a unique life of our own
tangential to the other, 'serious' one.
The antique rural identity dies hard;
also religion, and the widely shared
exceptionalism everyone likes to claim.
If these sustain us in the years to come
sure we'd be more at peace in our own minds
with no need for Angrian vulture funds
to solve our difficulties and make them worse:
if the bold Cubans could do it, why not us?

Not the most obvious choice, and Dublin 4
would shudder at the thought. So much the more
reason to think it at this critical time
of world coercion, multinational crime,
the feral capitalism and climate change
so many take as only natural. Strange,
only the imagination can set us right
and that means poetry, some version of it.
I hope this blather doesn't sound too trite.
Confident that we're on the same page, though,
I'm going to send it anyhow; and so
thank you for your panache and fortitude,
with all good wishes for the years ahead.

1/12/19

Acknowledgements

Five of these poems appeared in *Atlantis* (with artwork by Sarah Iremonger), published by The Gallery Press in a limited signed edition in March 2019.

Acknowledgements are due to the editors of *Archipelago* (Andrew McNeillie) and *Poetry Ireland Review* (Colette Bryce).